# Breaking Bread

**BUILDING
MEANINGFUL RELATIONSHIPS
FOR
LONG-LASTING
SUCCESS**

## Gautam Ganglani

Breaking Bread
Copyright © 2020 Gautam Ganglani
First published in 2020

ISBN
Paperback: 978-0-6487911-3-3
E-book: 978-0-6487911-4-0
Hardcase: 978-0-6487911-7-1

All rights reserved. No part of this book may be reproduced, stored in a retrieval system, or transmitted by any means (electronic, mechanical, photocopying, recording, or otherwise) without written permission from the author.

Because of the dynamic nature of the Internet, any web addresses or links contained in this book may have changed since publication and may no longer be valid. The information in this book is based on the author's experiences and opinions. The views expressed in this book are solely those of the author and do not necessarily reflect the views of the publisher; the publisher hereby disclaims any responsibility for them.

The author of this book does not dispense any form of medical, legal, financial, or technical advice either directly or indirectly. The intent of the author is solely to provide information of a general nature to help you in your quest for personal development and growth. In the event you use any of the information in this book, the author and the publisher assume no responsibility for your actions. If any form of expert assistance is required, the services of a competent professional should be sought.

**Publishing information**
Publishing, design, and production facilitated by Passionpreneur Publishing,
A division of Passionpreneur Organization Pty Ltd, ABN: 48640637529

www.PassionpreneurPublishing.com
Melbourne, VIC | Australia

Company Name: Digitalks
Founder: Raashi Sharma
Quotes designer: Raashi Sharma

# Table of Contents

| | |
|---|---|
| Foreword by Marshall Goldsmith | v |
| Prologue | x |
| What Is Breaking Bread? | 1 |
| Purpose: Why I Do What I Do | 5 |
| 5 Strategies to Break Bread | 15 |
| • Business Brews—Breakfast and Coffee | 15 |
| • Boost Meaningful Relationships | 20 |
| • Bring Tangible Value | 33 |
| • Build Strategic Partnerships | 41 |
| • Build Value Online | 49 |
| Affirmations—What Is the Value of an Affirmation? | 75 |
| Right Selection Speakers—Twenty-Five-Year Journey | 81 |
| Appreciation—Gratitude Is the Best Attitude | 87 |
| Testimonials | 93 |
| My Top 10 Books That Have Inspired Me To Break Bread | 105 |

# Breaking Bread engages & inspires positive action

GAUTAM GANGLANI

# Foreword

The final weeks of the year are a sacred time for many communities and cultures, when Indians celebrate Diwali and those in America celebrate Thanksgiving.

Though there are cultural differences between the East and the West, there is one thing you can almost certainly count on: a celebratory meal.

When we gather together to enjoy a meal, we are engaging in a tradition as old as humanity—one that transcends national borders and cultural divides.

What is it about food that brings us together?

While some may see it as a basic necessity, food promotes community. Our society segments and separates us in every way possible—by race, by class, by ability and education—something amazing happens when we sit down together to share a meal. Gathered around a table, we are all equals. Through the ingredients on our plates, we share a common connection to the Earth and to each other. Breaking bread together breaks down barriers and builds connections.

Breaking Bread

Several organizations around the world have recognized the enormous social value that comes from community meals. When it comes to personal branding and marketing, you can have the best technology, the most innovative marketing campaign, or the latest product, and it can all disappear overnight.

In today's world, all business success is interim. If you are a leader, the only competitive advantage you have is the combination of hearts and brains—yours, your people, your business partners, and your customers—that can produce happiness and success again and again.

I, too, have experienced the beauty of connection, great conversation, and spontaneous laughter flowing during a meal infused with the spirit of welcome.

This gives me great joy because of its simplicity as my wife Lyda and myself have enjoyed hosting dinners at our homes with family, friends, and even the MG Community, and we sit together at one long table and build belonging.

This year, as you sit down to enjoy your holiday meal, I hope you will take a moment to marvel at the vast web of life that connects your plate to your neighbors', and each of us to our bountiful and beautiful world.

I hope that, despite the stresses of the season, you will approach this occasion with gratitude—for the company

Foreword

you keep, for the food you consume, and for the vital and vibrant Earth that produced it.

And if you find yourself with an extra place at the table, I hope you will extend an invitation to a neighbor. Food may nourish your body, but community will nourish your soul.

As you read this book by my dear friend and business partner, Gautam, you will be startled out of your old conditioning by a whole new set of possibilities of you breaking bread to build meaningful, lasting, and loyal professional friendships.

I have had the pleasure of breaking bread with Gautam, be it a home-cooked meal at his place in both Dubai and Mumbai to celebratory dinners together in various countries in Europe, Gulf, and Asia exploring the local cuisines.

Are you ready to change the way you build relationships with the people who matter in your life personally and professionally?

Life is Good.

Marshall Goldsmith

#1 Leadership Thinker, Coach, and Speaker

Breaking Bread

*"Gautam is a fantastic relationship builder in multiple ways. As a business partner of mine, he has been a great partner.*

*We've always had a positive relationship. He's listened to me and not only focused on the client's needs or my need but also in terms of building client relationships and always looking to do what's right and not just what's expedient.*

*A guy who goes out of his way to really focus on what the client needs and how can I work with them. He builds a positive relationship and really gets to know them so that I can do a great job of delivering what they need. It's not an easy job, balancing the needs of the supplier (like me, a speaker), and the needs of a client.*

*So, Gautam is a really great guy and a fantastic relationship builder. Thank you, Gautam!"*

> # Breaking Bread is a positive energy exchange between two or more people

GAUTAM GANGLANI

# Prologue

From a very young age, my brother Jay and I always looked forward to a family meal together where we could share our experiences, learnings, and observations.

While both of us were busy with our lives, this quality time spent together was priceless, as it helped strengthen our relationships, build trust, and facilitate a positive exchange of energy between us.

Hence, the valuable lessons learned over meals have been a part of my formative years.

Throughout my professional life, I made deep friendships and built powerful relationships with people from multiple industries and various cultural backgrounds across the globe.

The idea of "Breaking Bread" is also an integral part of this professional journey and experience.

Wherever I am, I enjoy building friendships, collaborations, and partnerships. What better way to achieve that than by sharing a meal?

*Families that EAT together,*

*STAY together.*

*— La Motte*

# Breaking Bread is all about human connections

---

GAUTAM GANGLANI

# What Is Breaking Bread?

Breaking Bread refers to sharing a meal with someone, in the traditional sense of the phrase. However, this expression means more than just eating—it is sharing a sense of camaraderie with an individual or a group of people. It is a significant event that fosters meaningful connections and cooperation with a positive exchange of energies.

If you come across people who seem difficult to deal with, breaking bread with them demonstrates a sense of forgiveness and moving forward with positivity.

Today, people use the phrase *"break bread with someone"* when talking about sharing an emotional experience along with their food.

It is usually a gathering of some sort, as can be observed in the following situations:

- All the members of the community broke bread together and shared ideas on how to improve the area.

- The two leaders met and broke bread, and they forged a partnership between their two companies to co-create and collaborate.

Summary

The phrase *"break bread with someone"* is used to share a meaningful connection over a meal, often bringing together two people or groups to establish trust and rapport, and to explore areas for collaboration for mutual benefit.

*"There is something profoundly satisfying about sharing a meal. Eating together, breaking bread together, is one of the oldest and most fundamentally unifying of human experiences."*

*— Barbara Coloroso*

# Breaking Bread builds your Immunity, health & resilience

GAUTAM GANGLANI

# Purpose: Why I Do What I Do

All along, my journey has been driven by a purpose, a mission that I took on my own, owing to my personal struggles.

I was born and brought up in London. At the age of thirteen, I was bullied, teased, and humiliated in my school. This was a very challenging experience for me, and it affected me greatly.

I had practically no confidence, my self-esteem plummeted, and I felt like a total failure.

I could hardly make any friends. I became reticent, a recluse. Naturally, my grades fell below average, and nothing made any sense. I wondered what life was all about.

I went to my father, and I said, "Papa, I have very few friends, everything seems very negative, and my grades are poor. Where am I going from here? What's the purpose of my life? I can't make any sense of it."

He reflected on this and said, "Son, I'm going to give you three pieces of advice that will help you for the rest of your life."

Those were as follows:

1. **Surround yourself with the right people.** Being with like-minded and like-hearted people will uplift you, give you positive energy, and help you be happy. When you have a challenge, the right people will help you focus on the solutions and think positively.
2. **Devote time to continuously learning.** Develop yourself by reading as many books on personal development, listening to audios, and watching videos of highly successful people to get inspired.
3. **Last but not least—take action.** When you take action, you learn. You might succeed or fail, but you will gain experience along the way.

I started following my dad's advice and started feeling much better. At the age of sixteen, the opportunity came up to change schools and I was quite confident and excited about shifting to a new environment.

At my new school, I quickly connected with my classmates and very soon had a new set of friends. Because of my positivity, they were very friendly, warm, and supportive.

This boosted my self-confidence. Very soon, I started enjoying my life and became very proactive. I realized I was

## Purpose: Why I Do What I Do

now the person organizing events, parties, and weekend activities and very easily made more and more friends. My grades also improved as I scored above-average marks. This made me realize that just because I surround myself with the right people, I learn from my mistakes and their experiences and take the right action, and that helped me progress in my life.

So, when one of my coaches, Phil Bedford, told me, "While you do what do you, realize that each one of us has to go through life's challenges. It could be health, financial, relationship, or any obstacles. But when you surround yourself with the right people, you learn and take the right action. Then every challenge has a solution."

I realized this was good advice that helped me handle every situation in life because it is all about positive energy.

So the next time you face a challenge, think about surrounding yourself with the right people so you can learn from them. Read the right books, be it audio or video, and above all, take the right action that will help you progress or transform.

When I reflect on my life today, I see that my childhood journey made me realize that, be it personal or business, we all go through several challenges in life. However, as

Jack Canfield very clearly shared, Event + Response = Outcome.

Joining my dad Ram Ganglani in Right Selection in Dubai in 1995 was an opportunity for me to help people and companies transform their challenges and problems into solutions. The idea was to help them get from where they were stuck to transform their lives to where they want to be. The solutions would be to create events and experiences comprising world-class professional speakers and attracting like-minded professionals who appreciate learning and inspiring each other to take action and create new value in their lives.

This is why what I do excites and motivates me every day. The simple fact that every action I take will positively impact someone's life is motivation enough for me to rise from the bed every morning!

I share this picture with my dad as we are a "father and son" team.

This relationship has been built not just on a professional level, but on a personal level as well. One of my most precious times with my family is when we have a meal together.

Not just our family, but this holds true for other families as well. And this, friends, is what we culturally call "breaking bread."

Purpose: Why I Do What I Do

"Breaking Bread" is a term I was introduced to when I was in the UK as a child. It meant having a meal together that helps build better relationships, starting with your family.

Mealtime (usually the evening meal) is the ideal time for families to sit together and share their experiences of the day. Sharing dinner gives everyone a sense of identity. It can help ease day-to-day conflicts as well as establish traditions and memories that can last a lifetime. Conversations during the meal provide opportunities for the family to bond and learn from one another.

Over the meal, we are encouraged to start by sharing our successes of the day, what went well, etc. We then discuss the challenges each one is going through. The success stories trigger a natural appreciation of the effort put forth to keep the momentum going. Where challenges are encountered, this transparency shows openness and the willingness to learn from others. This triggers solutions and suggestions that we must be grateful for, without any obligation to follow them, but certainly review the same with an open mind. Such exchanges can be likened to "heart to heart" conversations whereby one person talks and the others focus and listen with empathy, with positive intentions.

However, the fast-paced life and influence of the global culture are taking us away from this custom. Fortunately, some recent studies have shown that even in developed countries, people are realizing the importance of family meals and are downshifting. It is indeed time to bring the "family" back to the dinner table.

To put it in a nutshell, eating together is an important social activity. That is why it has been said that "The family that eats together stays together."

The other challenge is the modern-day addiction we have fallen into, whereby even when we sit together for family meals planned with great effort, we distract ourselves with technology (such as mobile phones). We have to set strict rules/disciplines so each one is directed to keep their gadgets away and to honor and respect the time together.

When we were in Dubai, my dad and I also used lunchtime to break bread together in the office boardroom and always encouraged our core team members at the head office to join us whenever they could. The discussions were not strictly about business. We discussed personal issues like diet, health, hobbies, holidays, and daily news. This created a natural bond, while making our relationships better and stronger.

In the outside world, at social get-togethers and community gatherings, we usually hesitate to take the first step to connect. We live with misconceptions that the other person may not be interested in a conversation and that they may prefer to stay in their private space. This fallacy can lead to people becoming aloof and isolated, and developing low self-esteem when others do not connect with them.

I, therefore, believe that breaking bread with people in your community is a great ice-breaker, and this applies to all cultures. This is because we have common human emotions like the inclination to care and communicate, to help and support, to listen and learn, and to share our thoughts. Thus, offering a beverage, a cup of masala tea, a cookie, a sandwich, a mithai (Indian sweet), or chocolate is a great ice-breaker. Be the one to take that first step.

And now, going forth, there are a few more mantras I would like to share that will help in taking your personal or professional relationship deeper and making it stronger:

After mulling a lot over my journey and its learnings, I have shortlisted the best five tips that will help you boost and build your relationships while networking in the real world, as a professional and as an entrepreneur. I call them the *Business Conversations over a Meal*.

*"Breaking Bread is the best way to feel connected."*

# Breaking Bread works in person & virtually

---

GAUTAM GANGLANI

# Business Conversations Over a Meal

**Business Brews—Breakfast and Coffee**

The first meal of the day creates space for a conversation over a meal where there is an incomparable energy exchange. It helps break barriers between you and the customer and builds personal and professional relationships in meaningful ways.

Inviting a new contact or a potential client for a meal creates good conversation exchanges and breaks barriers between you and them. This is true not just for customers but for anyone with whom you want to have a growing relationship. It allows you to build authentic personal or professional relationships. Initially, each one of us has a wall or a barrier erected around ourselves, and we are not comfortable making new connections. However, once we learn the art of building relationships, we begin to enjoy the process.

In Dubai, for the last twenty-five years, we didn't have a dedicated sales team or even a sales executive in our entire organization. Ours was a unique situation, whereby our business model was (and still is) to run the business with a small close-knit team that is multi-talented and capable of multitasking. We have always relied on relationship-building and marketing. This led to us always dealing with in-bound and education-based conversations through which we grew and built our relationships.

I do not propagate that sales executives and sales teams do not have a role to play in the success of a business. In fact, they are an important part of the organization. However, when the marketing, business development, and relationship-building initiatives are done right, it makes the life of the sales team easier and helps skyrocket their performance, which ensures better results.

Let me share an anecdote with you. Food and friendship are a key part of the culture in the Middle East and India.

I know a dear friend who traveled from Dubai to Saudi Arabia regularly for over six months (seven visits). Eventually, it was only on the eighth trip when he met the client again that they signed a million-dollar training, consulting, and coaching deal that lasted for over two years.

My friend never gave up. His perseverance was incredible! Many presentations and consistent communication were shared. Most importantly, he noted they shared ten to twelve meals together.

Later, he learned that they used that time during meals to assess him, his attitude, and his behavior, and to learn about his cultural background. The client wanted to build a relationship and a certain comfort level with him before awarding him the contract.

This one deal gave him the belief that breaking bread together has a much higher value than he ever realized.

Breaking Bread is the number one strategy for building relationships.

I usually partake in six or more dinner get-togethers over twelve months with a group of potential clients. In 2009, when we were hit with the global recession, it was time to innovate and create new value. Yet, we managed to cover our costs. The loyal clients channeled a reasonable volume of business to Right Selection, even when they had a very tight budget.

**Here is the most popular question that people have asked me about my theory of Breaking Bread.**

**Question:** When we invite people to Break Bread, we are spending time and money without any assurance that the business will materialize. How does one sustain this?

**Answer:** Instead of money "spent," use the word "invested." Reframe your language, follow your budget, and keep an open mind. Do it with the mindset of investing time and creating value. Think with abundance, collaboration, and gratitude, and have no expectations. You are breaking bread with someone you might work with in the future. Over a meal, you will get a chance to listen to the other person's challenges and successes.

**Affirmations** (keep repeating to reinforce the message):

- Opportunities come with each door that I open, with each person that I meet.
- "Prosperity and abundance" is my natural state of mind.
- As I meet the needs of others, opportunity appears before me at every turn to take care of my needs also.

## Boost Meaningful Relationships

A relationship needs continuous nurturing, like a plant needs seeds, sunlight, and water.

In the same way, once you have established a professional friendship, you need to keep in touch for reasons that are not directly about closing a business deal. The goal is to build loyalty on top of the mind as you build an emotional bank account.

For example, on special occasions like birthdays or anniversaries (personal and work) send a personal note, voice note, or a picture on social media, and if appropriate, send a gift. The gift need not be an expensive item that has only materialistic value. What is appreciated is something that has a holistic benefit—for example, something that is educational or has learning value.

To build and boost relationships, we need to create loyalty. Therefore, on special occasions, it is a great idea to send a gift. This could be a signed book from a bestselling speaker, or even an invitation to attend a social or business event for which we may have access to complimentary seats.

**FAQ**

**Question: Can you share some stories of how you boost relationships?**

**Answer:** We send our clients a hamper of signed books authored by our popular speakers like Marshall Goldsmith and Ron Kaufman. Therefore, after every quarter, it prompts us to call them and have a conversation about what they learned and appreciated in the books.

When we host events, we also offer them complimentary seats. For instance, we had a total of 120 seats for an event. While most of the seats were sold commercially, there was a buffer of 20 percent seats for invitations. We used these to invite clients and prospects to enhance relationships and let them experience the business, content, and value before we discussed business.

This way, you have the energy exchange beyond the formality of business. Event invitations also include a meal, which is a part of hosting my first Breaking Bread.

At our seminars, it is vital to get like-minded people together to build relationships on an ongoing basis, do things differently, get close and add value, no matter what the business.

*"There cannot be relationships unless there is commitment, unless there is loyalty, unless there is love, patience and persistence."*

— Cornel West

Here is an anecdote to reiterate my theory.

**Indranil Chakraborty**

I was browsing on LinkedIn and came across some great content shared by an author and speaker named Indranil Chakraborty. I followed him for a couple of months and was impressed by the power of "business storytelling." He was constantly providing strong, valuable, and engaging content online.

One fine day, I felt the urge to reach out to him, so I sent him a message and said I would love to explore an opportunity to collaborate, and he was very receptive to it. We exchanged messages and phone numbers and set up a time to connect again around the third quarter of 2019.

In that conversation, we spoke about our base and locality, which happened to be Khar, Mumbai. We suddenly realized the magnitude of this coincidence. We were both staying within the same gated community. Unbelievable! We soon arranged to meet up at the business center a couple of days later and had the opportunity to get more familiar. After that, we went to a Starbucks nearby and, for the first time, we broke bread by having a cup of coffee over which we got to know each other better.

The next time, we met again at the business center in our complex. We spoke about an upcoming event with

Society for Human Resource Management (SHRM) where he was due to speak. I suggested that we collaborate and add tremendous value to his strategy and support his goals for that event, which we eventually did.

That relationship then led on to our hosting him in Mumbai and Bengaluru in January 2020 for a public program that he had put off for a couple of years because he did not have an event partner or logistics team to manage the whole project. That event was successfully hosted by us with a full house in both cities and resounding positive appreciation and feedback.

Indranil graciously invited me and my wife to dine and to meet his family. We also reciprocated the invitation. These were the interactions where I found someone like-minded and like-hearted, and we started a new professional-cum-personal relationship by breaking bread together.

I invited this one person to meet up over a cup of coffee, which led us to host an event, and that further led us to collaborate with him for strategic events in Dubai, Sri Lanka, and India and ultimately working together. Having a family meal at each other's homes again makes the relationship personal where you get to know each other more intimately. That's the journey of life.

Therefore, I encourage you to look out for stories of people online, especially when it is in the space that is directly correlated to your business. So, in social media or whatever platform it may be, be it LinkedIn, Facebook, or Instagram, look for like-minded people and approach them with genuine interest.

**Marshall Goldsmith**

About ten years ago, I connected with Dr. Marshall Goldsmith—a world-renowned author, speaker, and coach—and invited him to Dubai to do a presentation at a major event, specifically for the Government of Dubai.

I felt that the community in Dubai would also appreciate his work, so we organized a public seminar and focused on inviting coaches and corporate leaders. The event was a huge success. That led to a great relationship with Marshall, encouraging us to explore growing our collaboration together. Since then, we have had the opportunity to host him a few times in Dubai and the rest of the Middle East Region.

We have spent quality time together over meals or a cup of green tea, allowing us to know each other on a personal basis. He has also visited our home on a few occasions when he has had the time to unwind and has gotten to know the family very well. I have also had the pleasure of meeting his wife Lyda a couple of times at Thinkers50 in London.

This way, a fantastic relationship has been built over the years. After having proven ourselves as a great business house with trustworthy relationships, we exclusively represent Marshall Goldsmith in the Gulf, Indian subcontinent, and Africa.

During Christmas each year, he sends us a massive bouquet of flowers to both my parents and my team. So, there has been a constant exchange of energy over meals, exchange of gifts, and greetings on special occasions.

The last ten years have been amazing, as we represent one of the greatest speakers of all time, who is a humble soul, pays it forward, and makes a difference. He is someone whom I respect a lot.

At the last count, I realized we have crossed over fifty events with Marshall between public and private, and the relationship has been outstanding. This has built up during our multiple exchanges of conversations, both personally and professionally, and during flights or transit at airports in a dozen different cities.

## Affirmations:

- I always happily share positive messages and greetings to build and boost powerful relationships.
- My magnetic and dynamic personality connects me with the right people to start new meaningful relationships.
- I wake up every morning knowing I can create the ideal relationships for our businesses to mutually succeed and grow.

## Story of Passionately Breaking Bread

### First impressions

In January 2015, I had the pleasure of breaking bread with Moustafa Hamwi at Costa Coffee at the Dubai World Trade Centre, thanks to a referral by my coach and mentor, Phil Bedford. He thought there would be synergy between us, considering Moustafa's aspirations to become an international speaker, while we were the leading speaker bureau in the region.

Whilst we exchanged lots of positive ideas, it was apparent that it was premature for any collaboration, considering Moustafa was just starting his speaking career and we had a niche of working with international A-list speakers.

### Even a NO can become a YES!

Not long after that meeting, Moustafa took the opportunity to break bread with our chairman (my dad), whom he admired and highly respected. Also, this was triggered by a recommendation from our business coach at that time, Rajesh Nagjee, who believed Moustafa's "event industry" background would bring a lot of value to scale our seminar's side of the business. As Moustafa knew a lot more about our business from my first meeting, he was able to explore a different angle of collaboration, scaling up our business. Although this was not exactly what Moustafa hoped for on the speaking front, it was a great start to move from ideas into actually working together. This was discussed but mutually decided that the timing was not right.

**Third time lucky!**

A few months later, I met Moustafa again, and by that time, many more opportunities for the collaboration came into place for review. We both identified an opportunity we had not seen before. Until that time, we used standard MCs to open up for our A-list speakers at our events. However, with Moustafa's unique mix of experiences on stage and behind the mike, we realized there was an opportunity to add value to both.

We felt certain he could be the opening speaker at our events (an idea that came from his party-promoter days where a local DJ used to open up for an international DJ).

This gave us better quality content than a typical MC, helped us add a unique angle at our events, and gave him a platform to accelerate his speaking career.

In no time, Moustafa's opening talks became an "in-demand" fixture at our events and both of us enjoyed the fruits of this collaboration; yet this was only the beginning.

## Opportunities never end

As we both got to work together, we started jointly spotting further opportunities.

Content marketing was becoming a crucial part of event promotions: we already had a crew filming the event, and Moustafa had a strong media background. And this was the birth of Passion Sundays. What became one of the world's leading online talk shows about passion and one of our strong content marketing tools for our speakers in the region. This, in fact, was the first-ever online talk show led by a speaker from the Middle East, which gave a lot of leverage to all parties involved.

If this all sounds exciting, I can only tell you it was just the beginning. Since then, we have grown our businesses and personal relationships significantly.

For "Right Selection," we gained a strategic partner that had a complementing experience, which was crucial to our global growth: international events industry on a scale, media, PR, and content marketing along with a total passion for everything he does.

For Moustafa, he became one of the top speakers on his topic, commanding a rate card of $10,000 per talk, becoming ranked as one of the top one hundred coaches in the world by Dr. Marshal Goldsmith (actually he was the first-ever to be named so in the Middle East); he was nicknamed officially as "Mr. Passion" by Professor Tony Buzan; he co-authored a book with Brian Tracy and went on to conduct more than one hundred "face-face" Passion Sundays' interviews around the world, which built him a network of international A-list speakers. He now collaborates with them, which has led to his latest venture "Passionpreneur Publishing," one of the leading book publishers for speakers, coaches, and entrepreneurs.

**Final words, it's still just the beginning**

Today we are great friends and business partners. It started with the pleasure of surprising Moustafa and attending his Indian-style wedding in Kerala with the beautiful Diana (whom he met through other breaking bread opportunities within our business network).

Our collaboration has gone global through India, Singapore, and Australia, with many more countries to come. Our friendship and business collaboration is a book in itself. However, I share this story with you to understand, never to judge the first breaking bread meeting with someone, based on immediate results.

This is not to say that every single opportunity translates into collaboration; however, one thing for sure, we both create value for each other with a great understanding and respect of each other's strengths and different personalities. So even when the opportunities do not translate into actual collaboration, we still have the trust in each other's opinions and points of view.

To think all of this started at Costa Coffee with a meeting that looked like a "sorry nothing for us to collaborate on" only tells you one thing:

**Meaningful long-lasting relationships are built on breaking bread one step at a time, so plant the seeds, water them, and nourish them with lots of passion for what you do. What tree or what fruit, no one knows. The relationship is what is important.**

## Bring Tangible Value

When you meet customers or prospects to build relationships you, need to ask questions as a coach. "What's working for you?" Take written or mental notes. Be genuinely and authentically interested in the other person. Actively listen. As a general guide, we are given two ears and one mouth, so listen twice as much as you speak.

Whether it is a vendor, customer, or partner, take notes on what they share with open-minded questions. Learn something new from them so you can speak on multiple topics.

If we are unable to add value, then be honest and say no. Recommend someone else who can do a better job. This helps build trust between you and your prospective client.

Listen to their problems, make notes, and then prescribe solutions.

**Question:** Have you referred anybody? Has it backfired?

**Answer:** If you are not sure about referring someone, then do your research. I have a controlled endorsement of referrals. If it doesn't work, then be a solution provider. However, I can't recall such an instance.

**Question:** Have you got a situation when the customer just walked away with solutions, and you haven't built a relationship with the person?

**Answer:** YES! It is not a perfect world. These things happen. So, delete these experiences and move on. The person is just going to be a taker. I enjoy meeting people; I don't have to build a relationship with each one I meet. Focus on 80 percent of wins and take the balance 20 percent in your stride.

**Question:** How can we add tangible value to a friend, prospect, or customer?

**Answer:** When you go for an event, don't go alone. Take a friend along. This allows you to bond with each other during the event. In our busy schedules, the time spent together is like gold dust that you must create value from for mutual benefit.

At the event, you and your friend can talk each other up as people always listen more attentively when you speak positively about someone else rather than blow your own trumpet. Do you agree?

**Sports Personality**

In the first quarter of 2018, a dear friend of mine called me and asked, "Gautam, would you be interested in representing a sports personality?"

I replied, "I am very open to it if he is looking for representation as a speaker."

She said, "Yes. In fact, it's a cricketer. He and his marketing and branding partner are in town as he is playing a few cricket matches in the UAE. He is open to meeting with you if you are willing and available."

I said, "Absolutely! It will be my pleasure."

As an avid passionate cricket fan, I was all excited to meet the legend, so I arranged a meeting with him at the Shangri-La Hotel in Dubai. He came across as a very humble and approachable human being. We had a great conversation and explored ways where he has a business learning product in the training space and was looking to launch that in the Gulf and India for selective clients.

I suggested that we meet and dive deeper into the conversation and that I would love to invite him home for a meal. A month later, he was in town again, and I did invite him home for dinner, where we treated him to a home-cooked Indian meal comprising his favorite dishes—Butter Chicken, Paneer, and Dal. We also invited one of our closest friends' son, who was a cricket fan.

Over the meal, he and I had a great conversation where he also met my family. We started building a personal relationship while breaking bread together.

We then engaged him for a couple of events in Delhi and six months later again in August 2018. We kept in touch through the Indian Premier League (IPL).

So, that was a great opportunity where I met someone and broke bread with him in my home. Now, I have a direct connection with one of the greatest cricketing legends, and who knows where that will lead, for either of us.

*"The sharing of food is like breaking bread, it's very symbolic."*

*— Robert Irvine*

## Ron Kaufman

Over twenty years ago, in Dubai, UAE, I had the pleasure of meeting a speaker, Ron Kaufman. I first saw him when he was delivering a program for the Emirates International Bank. During his presentation, I recall him showing a motivational video clip about "A Bug's Life," which was about team-building and internal customer service.

Since then, we have had the privilege of hosting Ron Kaufman for several engagements in the entire Gulf Region and the Indian Subcontinent. As I look back now, I could see that we have hosted him for over a hundred events, be it public seminars, workshops, in-house private client events, and conferences since we first met.

Today, Ron is a very dear friend, my coach, and my mentor. He is someone for whom I have the highest level of respect, as he is a wonderfully loving, warm, and caring human being. Not only that, but Ron is also passionate about making a difference in people's lives, both personally and professionally, by providing them educational content and knowledge in the area of customer service experience through his brand, Uplifting Service.

We have had Ron home for dinner with his wife Jen several times in Dubai. I've also had the pleasure of being hosted by Ron, Jen, and their daughter, Brighten, in their Singapore home. where they have lived for over twenty-five years.

Ron is now part of my extended family, as he's also met my family members, including my parents and my brother's family.

In fact, he was even there in Dubai when my first daughter, Ambika, was born. He was generous enough to send a unique gift for her: a six-month supply of Pampers.

We have always been there for each other, not only during the highs and peaks when Dubai was booming, but even during the lows and difficult times during the global downturn. Ron is someone I can reach out to any time, any day (except when he is flying or on stage), and he's been a rock-solid pillar of strength in my life.

We have enjoyed conversations over several meals in different countries whenever we have traveled for events or conferences together. We have ensured we had meals together and took time to understand what was working for us, what were our challenges, and that our families were well and progressing. Sharing personal and professional stories has helped build a profound relationship.

Therefore, while it is definitely a business relationship, the foundation of this bond is the phenomenal personal relationship we have built on several occasions by breaking bread together over the years. Yes, it is a priceless experience having the opportunity to break bread with one's partners, friends, and clients, because it is a positive exchange of energy over a meal.

## Affirmations:

- As I meet new contacts, I always think of ideas I could offer to help them along their road to more success and prosperity
- As I set my mind to bring tangible value to the other person, I receive my prosperity from both expected and unexpected sources.
- As I genuinely and authentically show interest and listen to the other person, my empathy creates the platform for us to connect and serve each other more happily.

## Build Strategic Partnerships

In every business, there are relevant associations that have your target market as an audience. I encourage you to first have clarity on your target market in business or identify friends who have similar interests.

For example, in my industry, event planners, conference organizers, and CHRO's are my target market.

There is an event industry body called the EEMA that has over two hundred event agencies registered with them. We exclusively work with customized strategies for them.

Start by building your personal brand on media. Look to provide content online/offline. Connect with influencers, talk about an event, and say how phenomenal the meeting was. Go online and connect with them. It works, and here's proof.

Once I heard from an industry friend that Bollywood actress Dia Mirza is a raving fan of world-renowned author Malcolm Gladwell. I sent her a tweet regarding the same, to which she replied. This was followed by an e-mail from her management agency, which resulted in a face-to-face meeting with her within three weeks of my tweet.

So, don't let any mental blocks stop you. Don't tell yourself what is possible and what is not. There are ample possibilities out there, but your mind is the magnet.

Here is an exercise. Make a list of five to ten people you want to meet, and try to connect with them.

**Prasenjit Bhattacharya, GPTW**

In February 2019, I attended an event in Mumbai organized by the *Outlook* magazine and hosted by its editor Mahalaxmi and her team. We had several of our speakers attending it, including Frederick Harren, Arthur Carmazzi, and a few others

It was a very busy day for me. I was managing three speakers who happened to be on-site and a few back-to-back meetings.

I realized that Akila Balasubramaniyan of Harvard Business School Publishing, India, was present at the event, and I was keen to connect with her. However, the only opportunity I had to meet her was during one of the breaks, so I went up to her when I got my chance. I knew her from the past when we had hosted Whitney Johnson the previous year for a book tour.

Akila was standing with a gentleman—Prasenjit Bhattacharya, the CEO of Great Place to Work (GPTW), India. I was thrilled to meet him. We shared a conversation over a cup of coffee.

I learned from him that in three weeks that they were hosting their annual GPTW event with an expected audience of over twelve hundred people, and they had one keynote speaker slot available.

I offered a solution and mentioned Dr. Marshall Goldsmith was going to be in town, in case he fits their requirement and time slot. He found it to be a good fit and that it would be a great platform for the company to host Dr. Goldsmith, but they wanted to close the slot quickly. He was also not sure that Dr. Marshall would be available at such short notice.

However, I asked him to share the date, and he mentioned it was February 19. Upon checking the calendar, I realized that it was exactly on that day that Marshall was flying in from Saudi Arabia and flying out to Delhi the next day, so he was available for that evening slot! After checking with Marshall, I confirmed with Prasenjit that we could move ahead and make it work. We also quickly found a win-win solution to resolve the issue of the commercials.

The collaboration with GPTW to host Dr. Marshall Goldsmith resulted in phenomenal feedback at the annual event. They again invited Marshall for their Chairman CXO Annual Event in June.

We then went on to partner with GPTW for their Best Employees Club, which takes place quarterly. A year later, we have forged a great friendship and collaboration built on trust, abundance, sharing, and making a difference—which we call a givers' mindset.

We realized the power of corporates and entrepreneurs collaborating, whereby GPTW and Right Selection are forging a brand-new entity starting April 2020. All this started over a cup of coffee at an event a year back, and it led to a phenomenal friendship. We have had several meals together with our spouses and common friends. It is so much more fulfilling when we have a meal together and break bread with like-minded friends. There are unlimited possibilities.

**Achal Khanna, SHRM**

Society for Human Resource Management (SHRM) is one of the largest associations of HR professionals in India. Achal Khanna, a highly passionate, dynamic, and dedicated individual, is the CEO of this global association. From my experience, she is someone who knows how to make things happen, create value, make a difference in people's lives, and impact companies positively along their journey of growth and expansion.

I had the pleasure of meeting Achal at a couple of SHRM's programs here in India. I recall an occasion when our company, Right Selection, was hosting Dr. Marshall Goldsmith in Mumbai. Knowing how much she would appreciate the opportunity, I connected with Achal and invited her to have an exclusive interview with Dr. Marshall Goldsmith.

She obliged and attended the event at Sahara Star in Mumbai in 2019. There, we had the opportunity to bond over a cup of chai and biscuits and got to know each other better. Since then, Achal and I have kept in touch and constantly keep exploring ideas to identify where we could collaborate by providing speakers that would add value to the SHRM Conferences and Round Tables.

As she is based in Delhi, I shared with her my desire to meet her again and spend time with her when she next visited Mumbai. And, sure enough, shortly after that conversation, I got a call from her saying she was planning to visit Mumbai and proposed that we have lunch together and have a conversation on how to co-create projects for the benefit of the community.

We met up over lunch at the ITC Hotel in Mumbai in the middle of 2019.

SHRM is an association that we know targets HR professionals, and with Achal being the CEO of SHRM, it was just a pleasure having a meal with her and getting to know each other personally and professionally, making it more enjoyable for us to work together on upcoming projects.

Since that day, we have collaborated on several projects together, including bringing Lisa Ray with THRIVE Global

India to the SHRM Annual Conference in Delhi and another speaker named Shawn Dubravac.

So, it is great to meet like-minded and like-hearted people like Achal Khanna, who believe in collaborating, co-creating, and synergy. We are now great friends and are always happy to catch up over breakfast, lunch, or dinner, whenever the opportunity arises in Mumbai or Delhi.

Our company, Right Selection, now has a great partnership with SHRM. Going forward, we are looking to grow from strength to strength in 2020 and beyond.

## Affirmations:

- Success and good fortune flow toward me in a river of abundance, as I work on building win-win partnerships.
- To build powerful partnerships, I always project myself as an example of success and triumph.
- As I take the first steps toward creating tangible value for my clients and friends, all kinds of good things begin to flow in our direction.

*"The whole barrier exists because most people never come together and sit down at a table— join together, break bread together, and celebrate their differences and their likenesses"*

*— Oprah Winfrey*

**Build Value Online**

Optimize the power of social media.

Be active on social media, and build goodwill by exchanging value or positive energy by calling someone who is not well or on birthdays and anniversaries.

Build relations on social media. For instance, I mentioned how I connected with Dia Mirza with one tweet. The response one receives could lead to a meeting that would help take the business forward.

Share whatever expertise you have on social media through webinars and interviews.

Are you sharing articles, blogs, or webinars? Try using the concept of breaking bread as a strategic tool to build business.

To break bread, give out a book where content is the most essential. Give real value by selecting a relevant book.

**Shaheen Bhatt**

One day, while browsing Facebook, I came across a video about the book launch of Shaheen Bhatt (actress Alia Bhatt's sister).

The video featured Shaheen Bhatt, Alia Bhatt, and their parents Mahesh Bhatt and Soni Razdan, wherein they were being interviewed about Shaheen's book. The book was about her coming forward and sharing her story on how she dealt with depression from a very young age. It was about her painful journey throughout those years, and the launch was her "coming out in the open and sharing her diary and many other experiences."

She shared how she and her family realized the triggers that were helping her release the pressure.

The topic of mental health and well-being is omnipresent in people's minds globally since the last three years, and India is no exception.

So, when Great Place to Work (GPTW) was planning to host their annual conference and were looking for a speaker on the same topic, I decided to reach out to Shaheen Bhatt.

I reached out to my contacts and network from the events industry to connect with her. One of them replied saying she has a common friend who knows Soni Razdan and could get me the number. She was kind enough to get me the number, after which I called Soni Razdan and congratulated her on the launch of Shaheen's book. I then shared with her about our event in February at GPTW and how I would like to invite her daughter Shaheen to be one of the speakers at the event. She invited me to send an e-mail, which I did, inviting Shaheen to speak at the Conference on Mental Health and Awareness, and she promptly responded.

Things started moving when, one morning, I was browsing the Soho House app where I am a member. I learned that Shaheen was speaking a few days later to launch her book. I promptly registered for the event without a second thought and went along with my wife to attend the event. Before the event, I approached Shaheen and told her that I had sent an e-mail to her mother about a special event that we are hosting to raise awareness for mental health amongst our corporate clients in India. I then asked for ten minutes of her time after the session, which she kindly accepted.

During the event, I asked a couple of really good questions so that she could see me add value to the session. When we met after the event, she was very warm and forthcoming to have the conversation. I spoke to her about the GPTW Conference, and she shared that despite her being very keen to support and be there, she needed to check her schedule. A week later, she confirmed that she had managed to adjust her schedule and was willing to speak at the GPTW Conference. We confirmed everything, and I arranged for GPTW to order over a thousand copies of her book to be gifted to all the delegates and voila she was on board!

Now, we are connected on WhatsApp and looking forward to doing this event plus exploring many more opportunities in the year to raise awareness about mental health, so people can feel comfortable, come forward, and know that there are like-minded people and that they are not alone.

For me, this is a great example of finding something relevant on social media and finding a way (through my connections) to connect to and build a rapport. And here, she spoke at our event at GPTW, addressing twelve hundred people.

This, for me, is a wonderful example of making things happen by being aware, proactive, and positive, and believing that one finds a way to connect with the right person at the right time when you have the right context to approach them.

"It's the one thing you can control.
You are responsible for how people remember you—or don't. So don't take it lightly"

— Kobe Bryant

## Ashish Vidyarthi

I had the pleasure of interacting with Ashish Vidyarthi, Bollywood actor and speaker on Leadership and Motivation over the last three years since 2016 since I was visiting India.

I have seen him on several platforms People Matters, SHRM, NHRD, and numerous other conferences in India, and over that time, I always had the pleasure of listening to his high energy and engaging—in fact, inspiring—storytelling around various subjects from leadership to HR best practices. At each event, I took the opportunity to interact with him during the breaks over a cup of tea and even lunch.

We kept in touch over e-mail, social media, and phone conversations, and finally, in 2019, we invited him to Dubai to speak for the International Chartered Accountant Association of India. And he delivered fantastic high-energy? speaking engagement to over a thousand Indian professional delegates. The feedback was outstanding and very well received by the organizers, with the Vice-Chairman Anish Mehta giving a world-class testimonial of the energetic delivery style and high-value content.

That evening was a free evening for him, and I asked him if he would like to have dinner together in the hotel. He said yes to dinner but instead suggested we go enjoy street food, by which I was pleasantly surprised.

The most renowned place in Dubai is Ravi Restaurant in Satwa, so Ashish, myself, and my wife Panna had an enjoyable evening breaking bread over yummy street food at Ravi's. The kind of conversation we had spanned from family and education of our children to the market in the Gulf and India, and the fact that we were exploring the possibility of moving to India to grow our business. It was a thoroughly enjoyable relaxing informal evening in a casual restaurant with conversations like we were family friends.

This experience allowed us to really get us to get to know each other even more personally and professionally and build what I call a solid foundation and relationship. I only see positive interesting updates in the near future where our business will grow together with Ashish in 2020 and beyond.

**Gautam's Personal Fitness**

After moving from Dubai to Mumbai in July 2019, one of the things I wanted to get in order was my health and fitness. While I am not a person who enjoys going to the gym, I do believe that having a coach in every area of one's life that one wants to improve in works well.

As Dr. Marshall Goldsmith, the premier leadership thinker and coach in the world says, "A coach is someone who makes you stay accountable and adjust the behaviors you'd like to tweak, otherwise we lose our discipline and focus."

So, I realized that while I could have a business coach or a personal coach, a coach in the space of fitness was something that I needed. I thus took the time to look out for a gym trainer.

One morning, as I was walking around our pool, I noticed a trainer in our gym coaching some people. I went across and asked him, "How busy are you? Would you like more clients?"

He said, "Of course. I would appreciate any referrals you can share with me."

I replied, "It would be my pleasure, and I will keep it in mind."

That started my journey into taking and practicing physical fitness seriously.

And now, I have been working with my fitness coach for the last two months. I've been training thrice a week in the gym. My improved fitness has given me the confidence to start playing cricket, one of my favorite games, once a week. I have also started swimming regularly in our pool to improve my stamina. And finally, I now also participate in the Bollyfit dance classes to keep the fun in fitness.

Overall, getting back into a fitness regime has been an amazing move for me, giving me a great variety of exercises to keep me fit and at top energy at all times.

My coach recently reminded me that he had space and time for a few more clients. Recently, when I happened to be at our local salon for a haircut, while waiting for my turn, I started chatting with another lady. I don't recall how it came up in the conversation, but she mentioned that she was looking to help her husband get fit and healthy and even for herself, though she needed to be careful about what exercises she could do.

I asked her if she wanted a reference of my gym trainer, and she readily agreed.

It was my pleasure to provide a referral, and a week later, my trainer thanked me profoundly. He said this new client was on board and was very happy. So, this was a great scenario and opportunity where you help someone who is not helping you by connecting them to someone beneficial to them.

It is important to be aware of where one can have a positive exchange of energy.

Today, whenever that lady and the trainer meet me, they are both thankful because I thought of them and offered them something they were looking for.

Breaking Bread

The lady has now told me that she would love to have me and my wife home for dinner. This is how things move. Imagine that one has helped two people who want to reciprocate by inviting us home for dinner.

So, look for an opportunity to help others but not only for the results.

Be kind, be thoughtful, and share your appreciation with people. These gestures of goodwill will help you go a long way.

## Affirmations:

- To build lasting value for my new connections, I share only lucrative, enjoyable, and beneficial proposals.
- Success and achievement are natural outcomes for me, whenever I meet people with a mindset to provide them with something of lasting value.
- I am becoming better at building lasting value for others, as I have the power to do the most incredible things.

## HOW DO YOU BREAK BREAD?

All this begins with the simple idea of breaking bread. Amazing relationships are built over a chai, toast, coffee, or a simple meal. Use the concept as a relationship-building tool to find a way to add maximum value in the life of others and oneself.

It is highly possible that a certain portion of potential readers may not be the most adept at interacting freely with a relative stranger, and they would benefit significantly from a more thorough instruction regarding the same.

Are you someone who finds it a challenge to freely interact with a relative however relevant stranger?

Let me start by saying you are not alone. Many of my personal and professional friends have appreciated the fact that I can comfortably and confidently approach strangers to build rapport, even secure a meeting or positive commitment to solve a challenging situation be it at airports, hospitals, restaurants, events, residential elevator, or even on flights at thirty thousand feet in the sky.

Below are some simple actionable ideas, which I suggest for your positive consideration to build rapport and break bread by having a positive energy exchange with another human being that have worked for me:

1. Smile
2. Good Morning
3. How are you?
4. I need your help
5. How long have you been in this industry?
6. What have you enjoyed most about your profession?
7. How is your family?
8. What are your hobbies?
9. What is your favourite food?
10. What is your favorite holiday destination?

You need to greet someone with warmth and a genuine greeting as a start.

Then select one or two open-ended questions depending on the person, location, and situation. This will invite the opposite person to share. As they share, they will feel appreciative of you actively listening and more than likely ask you a similar question allowing you to share.

Depending on the situation, location, and timing you will then ask for a contact, meeting, solution, or simply appreciate their valuable time, so you build a positive impression until you meet again.

## The Power of Asking

Overcome your subconscious fears with **Gautam Ganglani, Right Selection Speakers** as he shares his insight on taking charge and creating possibilities.

"Have you ever hesitated to ask?"

Well, you are not alone. A lot of friends I know always hesitate to ask.

I have a great story and example to share with you. Recently I was in Delhi, and I had a flight booked at 9:00 p.m. from Delhi to Mumbai. I arrived at the airport much earlier than my scheduled flight. I noticed that an earlier flight for Mumbai was scheduled to take off in around fifty minutes.

I was traveling with a few friends. I told them I am going to go and ask if we can take the earlier flight. They said it's not possible and that it's only fifty minutes for the flight to take off and we would have to pay extra and then we don't know if we will get seats, etc.

I said ok leave it with me. I approached the airline desk and found out who oversaw the flight and I said to him, "I need your help!"

And the next question he said is, "How can we help you?"

"Well, I am booked on the 9:00 p.m. flight, but I would like to leave on the earlier flight to arrive home earlier and catch up with my family and would appreciate it if you can help me and my two friends get on that flight."

Within a few minutes, they said to us, it is done. Three seats taken care of. I alerted my friends, and we rushed to get on that flight.

My friends still wonder and ask me, "What did you say or ask?"

This is something I do naturally, because the worst that can happen is you will get a *No*! But by not asking you are rejecting yourself in it being a 100 percent *No*!

When you ask, the chances of approval are at least 50 percent.

So, I recommend next time you are stuck in a situation where you need help or support, be confident and comfortable to ask. I recommend you apply that in your professional and personal life.

## BREAKING BREAD IN A VIRTUAL WORLD

Little did I know, or could I ever imagine, that my book *Breaking Bread* that you are reading will need an additional chapter to be included before it is published.

Today, April 2, 2020, I planned that my book *Breaking Bread* will be published and launched later this month in the presence of two of the greatest speakers in the world, Marshall Goldsmith #1 Leadership Coach and Ron Kaufman #1 Customer Service Guru during a series of events in Dubai, Mumbai, Bangalore, and Colombo.

However, COVID-19 had its own plans to disrupt the world and have over a billion people in lockdown for twenty-one days and globally over a hundred countries following suit. Coronavirus created a global pandemic resulting in anxiety, confusion, stress, and disruption with uncertainty about what is in store for the world.

My family and I were scheduled to travel to Dubai for my wife's father's seventieth birthday celebration on March 16, and we had three events with speakers scheduled. However, on March 11, the government announced travel restrictions to re-enter the country until April 15, so we decided as a family to cancel our plans to visit Dubai, and all business events were postponed or canceled.

## Business Conversations Over a Meal

This was a difficult decision for us because being a close-knit family, my daughters were looking forward to their holidays with grandparents, time with family and friends, and to visit their favorite places in Dubai—it being their city of birth where they spent many years of their childhood days. But we knew this was the right decision to take as a family to stay together in our home in Mumbai as one thing we were sure about was the situation was going to get worse before getting better.

Learning from my dad's three principles he shared with me in my teenage years, which I shared in the earlier part of this book, I decided now more than ever before in my life I needed to apply those principles.

1. Surround yourself with the right people
2. Continuously learn
3. Take action

In the past, at different times in my life, I have had business, relationship, financial, and health challenges. However, at this stage, I was presented with all four challenges simultaneously, as I am sure many people are facing at the moment.

Seeing all the global news on WhatsApp from family and friends was disheartening, disturbing, and shocking. It starts affecting one's mindset. Whilst I consumed that content for a few days, I realized the saying, "We are what we consume." I recalled one of the best decisions I made in my life was to stop subscribing or reading a newspaper since January 2009. Now it was no different. I took an immediate decision to stop reading or sharing the negative news. I simply accepted that the situation globally is very serious, and there is not much I can do. So, I learned to trust the national leaders, the heads of security, and the heads of the medical fraternity to fulfill their responsibilities very diligently, which they surely did.

My responsibility was to stay home and stay safe with my family, keep hygiene, and create an ecosystem at home for my family's wellbeing.

Keeping my dad's advice in mind, I sat quietly and said to myself, "I cannot change what I cannot change; however, I have the power within me to choose how I use this valuable time to invest in myself for my future and make the world a better place to live in."

The words "social distancing" were shared time and time again during the lockdown; however, I reframed it immediately to the actual meaning, which was "physical distancing." We were presented with a great opportunity to socially connect with our family, extended family, team, current friends, and school friends, and create meaningful conversations and build quality relationships.

I took a blank notebook and wrote down more than a hundred names in my personal and professional life who I wanted to speak with. To see how they are with their families and to ensure they are safe and well at home. Then, to explore ideas of how best we can use this time to ensure stability as a family and then create a day structure that covers relationship, health, business, and finance.

Each day, I called three to five people from this list and enjoyed the conversations as they were meaningful, uplifting, and encouraging. Even for those who were in a negative mindset, I know each one felt positively energized, encouraged, and above all grateful, after the call.

My level of gratitude from this experience has gone up tenfold. This experience of being in our houses made every one of us realize that a roof over our heads, meal on the table each day, and good health are the ultimate gifts for which we need to be grateful.

**Learning**

Create a list of people you know, personally and professionally, to call, e-mail, message, or send a voice note to check how they are, share your gratitude, and explore ideas of how you can add value and possibly collaborate.

Have a Zoom call with your friends and family, and share stories and updates to positively energize each other.

Breaking Bread

Every Monday my team meets for our weekly huddle to review the status of business operations and sales to plan the activities and focus for the week ahead with an agenda to cover twenty or more items in a three-hour meeting.

Today, Monday, March 16, was different. I started by saying that business will slow down completely before starting again. This meeting will follow my favorite mantra, "less is more." We will cover only five topics thoroughly. There was no rush to complete an agenda. We needed to pause, slow down, reflect, and deeply discuss each topic so it was thoroughly covered.

I shared with the team that phase 1 is to plan for the next forty-five days until April 30, with no conversations about any commercial conversations as it was sensitive and inappropriate unless it was an inbound conversation by a client in need.

I asked the team the following questions.

What value can we create during these forty-five days that helps us break bread with our existing community and the community at large?

What can we achieve in these forty-five days?

What new can we learn in these forty-five days?

## Business Conversations Over a Meal

What can we do in these forty-five days that we have not had the time to do before?

From this conversation, we hosted four webinars in eight days and had over fifteen hundred? registrations with 60 percent attendance. We created meaningful conversations, built tremendous goodwill and appreciation, and grew our database of like-minded and like-hearted people who have a passion for continuous learning.

I started attending webinars being hosted by global thought leaders and regional speakers based on topics I wanted to understand better or learn how I can do things differently. This activity kept my mind fresh and filled me with an abundance of positive energy.

We can only give others what we have inside. This positive feeling of gratitude helped to add value to every conversation I had with people.

I started being even more active connecting with people socially on LinkedIn, Facebook, and Instagram. My LinkedIn followers grew faster as people had more time to connect with relevant content and people, to make new connections with common interests.

From numerous conversions I had with people during this valuable time at home, it resulted in me creating a Breaking Bread Ecosystem mentioned below.

Breaking Bread Book
Breaking Bread E-Book
Break Bread Audio Book
Breaking Bread Website
Breaking Bread App
Breaking Bread Webinar Series
Breaking Bread—Building Blocks CSR Initiative
Breaking Bread Podcast
Breaking Bread Blog
Breaking Bread Keynote Speech

So even when you are in a lockdown or maintaining distance and cannot have physical face-to-face conversations over a meal, you still have the opportunity to break bread virtually over social media and meeting platforms like Zoom where you can have a conversation and see each other to enjoy meaningful conversations.

What can I say except thank you for reading my book and I trust it has inspired you to surround yourself with the right people, continuously learn, and take action to enjoy more happiness and fulfillment breaking bread to build meaningful relationships for long-lasting success.

I invite you to visit www.gautamganglani.com and join our growing community of passionate, like-minded, and like-hearted people who are happy to have engaging conversations and build meaningful relationships.

**Are you ready to Break Bread?**

## Relationship Building Actionable Ideas by Gautam

1. Reconnect with one or two people every week. This week call a client or prospect you have not been in touch with for a while, a former business colleague, a former friend, and a current friend you haven't spoken with for a while.
2. Volunteer, write an article, or join a committee in your company. Becoming known helps you meet people and develop relationships faster and more profitably than just attending meetings.
3. Send one handwritten note a day. Send these to people in your network to say thank you, offer congratulations, send an article of interest, extend an invitation, or just to keep in touch. Use "found time" during the day to write these notes and make them short and simple. Carry note cards and stamps with you.
4. Write an article or newsletter to send to your contacts. This promotes your business and helps you keep in touch with your contacts. You can easily do this electronically.
5. Send gifts. Remember those who help you, or just remember a special occasion for those in your network. Develop a list of reliable vendors of unique gift items for these occasions.
6. Use "giveaways" that constantly remind the recipients of your name and your business. Look for useful quality items that will be appreciated and that will keep your name in front of others.

7. Follow up within twenty-four hours of a meeting to say "Nice to meet you," "Thanks for your time and consideration," and if appropriate, set another meeting.
8. Make a list of opening lines to use when meeting someone new. Use open-ended questions that require more than a one-word answer, or at least follow up with an open-ended question.
9. Develop an infomercial about yourself. Practice it until it becomes spontaneous and natural.
10. Smile when meeting people, entering a room, or talking on the phone. A smile is the first step in building rapport.
11. Listen with care. Be aware of what the other person is saying instead of thinking about what you will say next. You will remember much more about the person and the conversation.
12. Give compliments. Make a goal to look for positive attributes.
13. Make a list of the key people in your industry or profession that you would like to meet. Determine what organizations, places, and people they know to help you find a way to meet them.
14. Become a resource for others. Give generously of your time and expertise.
15. Develop a system to keep in touch with everyone in your network regularly. As your list grows, divide

## Business Conversations Over a Meal

it into categories and have a contact plan for each category.
16. Answer your phone and e-mail messages within twenty-four hours even when you are on the road. With today's modern technology, there is no reason to not be in touch.
17. Once a month, have lunch with a friend, colleague, or client you have not seen for a while.
18. At a company function, set a goal to sit next to someone new and get to know them.
19. Read publications. When you read a good article, send a compliment note to writers, journalists, or contributors.
20. Be courteous to everyone you meet, don't judge a person too quickly. In addition to being an important lifestyle choice, you never know who that person is connected to or when they may become your next important contact.

"

# Breaking Bread is about connecting personally with authenticity

---

**GAUTAM GANGLANI**

# Affirmations — What is the Value of an Affirmation?

**Ram Ganglani**

You have noticed a set of affirmations at the end of each chapter. I have always believed in positive thinking, affirmations, and creative visualization right from my childhood days, hence my passion for writing and sharing affirmations.

Let me explain what affirmations are, how they work, and what benefits they hold. I am also sharing a few more general affirmations at the end, so you can start building a stock of different affirmations to use, depending on the situation and challenges you are going through.

Often, a majority of the people are unaware of their strengths and weaknesses, even when others tell them about it. When mixed with negative phrases that you often use, such as, "What an idiot I can be!?" which, whilst it was supposed to have a positive effect, can actually result in negative consequences, the degree of the message and resultant programming into your subconscious can have hazardous results. What sets people apart are their attitudes about themselves, and this is where positive affirmations come into play.

**Positive Affirmations**

Positive affirmations are statements that assert the existence or truth of something positive. It can be achieved by programming your subconscious mind to believe that the truth exists, and the realization of this truth is favorable to your personal well-being. Positive affirmations are also described as a form of autosuggestion or self-hypnosis.

Positive affirmation is a very powerful tool that can be used to influence and change the way a person thinks or feels about himself, which translates into his attitude and actions when facing others. Positive affirmations work for everyone, as their very nature merely amplifies what we already have in our minds. These can be your attitudes, your thought processes, and anything else that runs across your mind. With insistent use of positive affirmations, you will be able to reprogram your internal subconscious mind, changing the negatives into the positives.

## Affirmations—What is the Value of an Affirmation?

One good way to remain positive is by constantly renewing our thoughts in our mind. The effectiveness of positive affirmations lies in its transformation into action. What makes it work is your confidence in it working. Similar to a self-fulfilling prophecy, by constantly saying it to yourself, the subconscious mind will make it become the truth. The most efficient way to go about doing so is by continuously sowing positive thoughts and nurturing them.

**Benefits of Positive Affirmations**

The primary benefit of positive affirmations is that it can be enforced to any and every portion of your life that you want to improve on. This can be about your career, health, relationships, or finances.

There are other benefits to using positive affirmations for the subconscious mind. People who keep affirming their minds with positive words and thoughts have stronger and more active muscles. On the other hand, if you give free rein to negative thoughts you often find themselves feeling tired.

Positive affirmations also influence your energy level, and a happy individual is usually one with many positive thoughts and programming. Hence, experts advise that it is beneficial to start every day with positive thoughts and words that will act as a multiplier on other aspects of your life as well.

Lastly, a positive affirmation allows you to fulfill your capabilities, strengths, and talents. By constant repetition, you will eliminate the feelings of doubt and insecurity that bother you, making it easier to achieve a positive result.

## My Selection of Ten Positive Affirmations Especially for YOU!

- I am always joyful and happy, no matter what happens every day.

- I keep doing what is good and what is right for all, and I stay at peak energy at all times.

- I meditate and exercise every day. I am now calm and peaceful, enjoying perfect health every day.

- I constantly stay in peak state as I contribute my time, energy, and wealth to all those in need, no matter at what level they are.

- Along with my colleagues, I am reaching greater and greater heights, while benefitting everyone along my journey.

- I feel truly at peace, as all my actions and decisions are securing a wonderful future for me and my family.

- My feeling of constant gratitude keeps multiplying all the blessings I am already enjoying.

- I always give my best in everything I do.

> # Breaking Bread is a Science & Philosophy that brings inner fulfillment

—— GAUTAM GANGLANI

# Right Selection Speakers — Twenty-Five-Year Journey

**Right Selection Speakers** is a "father and son" family business. If someone were to ask what business you are in, the common answer would be "publishing and providing public speakers." However, every business must have a mission, and ours is to transform lives through inspiring stories.

So, yes, I am proud to state that "we are in the business of transforming lives." What started twenty-five years ago as a corner bookstore for "personal development" literature has today evolved to become a "learning and development" talent powerhouse for corporates and conference organizers. Today, it gives me great pride to say that Right Selection Speakers is a life-transforming company.

The genesis of our business is my father Ram Ganglani's childhood passion for personal development. He derived great pleasure from reading inspirational books by bestselling authors like Dale Carnegie, Norman Vincent Peale, and Napoleon Hill and was immensely inspired by them.

He started his career by joining the family business in West Africa and then in Europe in 1965. In October 1993, after a long span of twenty-eight years, he was ready to follow his passion once again and transform his passion into a business concept. So, he moved away from the family business and ventured out to Dubai in the Gulf Region to open the first new-age Self-Help book store called **Right Selection**.

Soon after he opened the book store, I graduated, and my deep desire to be an entrepreneur prompted me to readily join the business in 1995.

Developed over ten years, the business was about creating value by transforming lives. We believed that through these books, we could catalyze everyone, no matter what challenges they were going through. We sold these powerful books through our retail store and also distributed to the supermarkets in the high streets, where the footfall was much higher than at the regular bookstores. What drove us to grow and reach out to more people was the very belief that these books could certainly impact many lives.

### Right Selection Speakers—Twenty-Five-Year Journey

In those days, speakers like Tom Peters, Philip Kotler, Stephen Covey, and Robin Sharma were visiting the Gulf for public seminars. Fortunately, we were invited to display our books at these events. Over time, we realized that we could take our business to the next level by taking the initiative of bringing these best-selling celebrity authors for live seminars and workshops.

The insight was that when people read a book and get inspired, they start looking at the author as a guru or mentor and want to meet the author in person.

So, we first started by selecting the authors whose books were selling in bulk. It meant people resonated well with the content of the book, as it would have helped them in some way, personally or professionally. Gradually, that was how the public seminar business started in 2000, and that led to large conferences.

Today, our company has a global speaker management service. Since we are also in Mumbai now, we promote Indian speakers locally as well as open global opportunities for them also.

Then, there is the consultation service, where we have the training side of the business such as mindfulness workshops.

This way, what started as a simple books service, went on to include in-house services and moved on to become a speaker bureau-cum-speaker-management consultancy.

The past twenty-five years have been full of passion and purposefulness, the credit of which goes to teamwork and perseverance in the face of good and tough times.

> **Gratitude & appreciation everyday is an integral part of Breaking Bread**

---

GAUTAM GANGLANI

# Appreciation—Gratitude Is the Best Attitude

The book *Breaking Bread—Building Powerful Relationships* was inspired by my family, friends, customers, business partners, celebrities, influencers, and all other well-wishers. Thank you for being the fuel to my fire.

I'd like to thank my parents, Ram and Shallu, for being my pillars of strength in my journey of life and always encouraging me to be the best version of myself.

I also thank my dear wife, Panna, for always being there by my side, sharing her positive energy and joy at all times. Her biggest contribution to my journey is helping me break bread by hosting over fifty dinners at our cozy home in Dubai.

I thank our two beautiful daughters, Ambika and Vivina, who inspire me every day to be the best father I can be.

Thank you to my brother Jay, his wife Divya, and their two children Sherina and Nikesh, for being great positive support at all times.

I am grateful to my parents-in-law Gulshan and Lata and family for their constant love, support, and blessings along my journey.

I would also like to thank all my team members who have been a part of my journey, especially my current senior team members Rinkesh and Bhavna.

I thank all the speakers I have interacted with over the years. Special thanks to Ron Kaufman, my personal friend of over twenty years, and Marshall Goldsmith of ten years.

I thank my coaches, which I have had many, from Phil Bedford, Rajesh Nagjee, Moustafa Hamwi, Himanshu Saxena, Karthik Narayan to Rajiv Talreja.

Thank you Moustafa Hamwi my publisher & dear friend Sohin of Embassy Books India for their wholehearted support, guidance & encouragement for my writing journey of this book, "Breaking Bread."

I thank my teammates of Marketing Mastermind, Payal, Raashi, Shashank, Indranil, and Amey, who have supported me in creating awareness of my book and helping the message reach people globally.

## Appreciation—Gratitude Is the Best Attitude

I have several other people to thank, including friends and associates whom I have met and interacted with and learned so much from. Thanks to each one of you for your contribution.

Last, but not the least, I am abundantly grateful to the powers above for bestowing the love, blessings, and grace all along my journey, which took me to different countries across the globe, with a special affinity to England, United Arab Emirates, and now India.

I hope this book will add value to your personal and professional life and you will gain deep insights into the proven theory of breaking bread.

**Are You Now Ready to Break Bread?**

From over twenty years of experience in building professional friendships with people who value meaningful relationships that go far beyond just business, I trust you have enjoyed reading my book with simple yet actionable ideas supported with true stories from my experience and that you are now ready to break bread with the people who matter in both your personal and professional lives and experience more happiness and fulfillment whilst enjoying the journey of life.

Breaking Bread

What does Breaking Bread mean to you?

How soon will you commit to breaking bread with someone in your professional network?

Can you list breaking bread with?

Will you write to me and share your experience of breaking bread?

### Appreciation — Gratitude Is the Best Attitude

In addition to having a meal what other ideas come to your mind when you think of breaking bread?

Are you ready to build meaningful relationships with your target audience?

Can you recall breaking bread in the past when it later turned out to be a success story?

In todays virtual world how do you plan to use the concept of Breaking Bread?

# Breaking Bread helps builds global cultural relationships

GAUTAM GANGLANI

# Testimonials

*"Gautam is fantastic at building high value, long-term partnerships, around the table and around the world."*

**Ron Kaufman:** World's leading educator and motivator for uplifting customer service and building service cultures

*"Gautam Ganglani brings energy, positivity, and a willingness to collaborate to everything he does. This book will inspire you to follow his lead."*

**Stuart Crainer:** Cofounder, Thinkers50 | @thinkers50 | thinkers50.com

*"Gautam Ganglani lives what he preaches in this valuable book about the value of breaking bread with people as a strategy for a more successful and fulfilling life in business. I have experienced the power of deepening our personal and professional relationships over meals in his home in Dubai and in restaurants all over the Gulf. I encourage you to read this book and apply its wisdom to your life."*

**Jack Canfield:** *New York Times* bestselling author of *The Success Principles and Chicken Soup for the Soul*

*"Working with Gautam on a number of business topics over the past dozen years, it is very clear that he is the master at building professional relationships, has a novel way of adding value in each situation, and is prepared to give everything to see success. Breaking Bread is a powerful book on the life learnings of sharing."*

**David Macadam:** CEO, Middle East Council of Shopping Centers and Retail

*"Gautam has been exceptional in his ability to quickly connect with people and build a lasting relationship. He is able to find common ground and comes from a place of helping and adding value first. If you want to decode how to build lasting and profitable relationships then read this book."*

**Neeraj Shah:** CEO and Founder, Titan Masterminds | Business Mentor

*"Gautam is one of the most genuine human beings I have ever met! And this trait is only further enhanced by his commitment to the noble vision of helping people to be more and do more with their careers and lives. In these lightning-paced lives that we lead, his philosophy of 'breaking bread' with the people you live, work and play with is certainly the call of the hour! It reminds all of us that no matter who we are, or what we are, it is the power of relationships we forge with our community that is instrumental in our success and more*

*importantly happiness. Thank you, Gautam, for inspiring us to 'break bread' with our loved ones more often."*

**Tanvi Bhatt:** Founder of Tanvi Bhatt International, India's premier personal branding company

*"Gautam is an awesome Connector and Entrepreneur. I first met him at Marshall Goldsmith's seminar in 2017 at ITC Hotel, Mumbai. His 'Breaking Bread' concept has inspired so many members of our Entrepreneur Excel community helping them to know each other better, build quality relationships with authentic sharing, accountability, and honest feedback."*

**Namrata Thakker:** Founder of Entrepreneur Excel

*"Your services are very impressive! Gautam, allow me to express that you are an anchor always willing to help out at anything that is needed. Your team's attitude is always very uplifting, and it really makes a difference when things get hectic."*

**Prasenjit Bhattacharya:** CEO, Great Place to Work Institute, India

*"It is always a pleasure working with you, Gautam. Through your vast experience, you demonstrate tremendous skills and conduct business in a very professional manner."*

**Achal Khanna:** CEO, SHRM India

*"I had the good fortune of connecting with Gautam more than a decade ago. Thanks to him, during my interactions I had the pleasure to connect with many global celebrities like Jack Canfield, Ron Kaufman, Marshall Goldsmith, and Allan Pease.*

*Gautam is a seamless connector. He has the knack of connecting the right people to each other. He is transparent, ethical, and very professional. I wish him all the best in his new role as the keynote speaker and author of* Breaking Bread.*"*

**Sampath K. Iyengar:** Chief Visibility Officer Neural Maven Community and Talk Show Host at Jam with Sam

*"Gautam is a passionate entrepreneur who builds high-quality relationships for long term success. It has been a pleasure to collaborate with him personally and professionally.*

*I am sure his book,* Breaking Bread *will add tremendous value to you in learning how to build meaningful relationships."*

**Ester Martinez:** CEO and Editor, People Matters

*"Breaking Bread is an important and often under-utilized trait in business success. People like to do business with other people they like. Investing time and*

*effort in building a strong relationship forms a strong foundation for success. Gautam Ganglani is truly passionate about Breaking Bread. I have seen him talk on this subject and watched how he conducts his life true to this concept. This book is a labor of love. I would strongly recommend you read it if you want to succeed in business and in life."*

**Kiruba Shankar:** Founder President, Professional Speakers Association of India

*"It has been a pleasure to know Gautam personally, and I have enjoyed his approach to building relationships based on creating value."*

**Miss Malini:** Founder and Creative Director, @missmalini

*"When it comes to the concept of breaking bread, I think Gautam is a great role model as he highly values relationships and enjoys collaborating for a win-win."*

**Marcus Ranney:** General Manager, Thrive Global India

*"Gautam is the networker of networkers. He is passionate about meeting and helping people in whatever way he can. He is a sincere and honest businessman determined to create win-win scenarios for all who do business with him.*

*For over ten years Gautam has successfully represented me, as a speaker and sales trainer, in the Middle East. He not only created great public events but introduced me to many corporate decision makers for conference keynotes and customized in-house sales training programs.*

*My success in the Middle East is because of Gautam's commitment to helping people succeed, through books, speakers, and trainers."*

**Bob Urichuck**

International Professional Speaker, Trainer, and Author. Founder of the "Buyer-Focused" Velocity Selling(.com) System

*"Gautam is a consummate professional who is passionate about adding value to his clients. I have seen him go that extra mile to ensure excellence and impact. This attitude of his toward work is inspiring. And that's the business we are in."*

**Ashish Vidyarthi:** Actor | Founder, Ashish Vidyarthi and Associates-Avid Miner Traveller

*"I have had the pleasure to collaborate with Gautam for over a decade and believe that the secret behind the longevity of this partnership is the integrity of character with which Gautam operates with his partners.*

*If anyone can legitimately discuss building meaningful relationships, it is Gautam, and I hope this book will be an invitation to its readers to develop a professional network in the same spirit of 'breaking bread,' one of contribution and sharing each other's resources to benefit to all."*

**Sophie le Ray:** Entrepreneur, Author, and Business Facilitator. Co-founder of Naseba

*"Gautam is a pleasure to work with and an excellent communicator, connector, and great at keeping, honoring, and growing relationships. He is filled with positive energy and believes in making things happen.*

*As a professional speaker, I have experienced his excellent rapport and ability to strike successful deals that are win-win for companies and organizations as well as for speakers. Right Selection continues to grow in markets like India and the Middle East, thanks to his commitment and passion for business. This is what has made Right Selection Speakers Bureau one of the best speaker's bureaus with relationships with world-class speakers and high-performing organizations.*

*I will wholeheartedly recommend him to all organizations as well as speakers for his professionalism as well as international exposure.*

*I wish him all the best and look forward to our continued positive association."*

**Yogesh Chabria:** #1 Bestselling Author | Founder, The Happionaire® Way | Entrepreneur | Speaker and Business Strategist

*"Gautam is an amazing person to work with. One of the best networkers I know and someone you can always rely on. It is an absolute pleasure having him as a partner, and I endorse him 500 percent as an ideal candidate to do business with. His pleasant personality, integrity, and understanding between the Asian and European cultures makes him a very special and valuable individual."*

**Ernesto Verdugo:** Author, Entrepreneur, International Public Speaker, Consultant, Accelerated Learning Practitioner, and Internet Coach.

*"Gautam and I agreed on a cross-mentoring collaboration at the beginning of my public speaking career. What I loved most about him is that he possesses over twenty years of experience in his field and still he is obsessed with learning more, improving, and adding more value to others. This proves to me that he found his passion for inspiring, connecting, and empowering*

*people. Thank you, Gautam, for always being straightforward, helpful, reliable, and genuine."*

**Dr. Natalia Wiechowski:** Personal Branding Strategist, Keynote Speaker, and Edutainer

*"Relationships are crucial to our success, no matter what we want to achieve in our business. Gautam is deeply passionate about building meaningful relationships with those he interacts with personally and professionally. You will be inspired to take action by reading his book,* Breaking Bread.*"*

**Keith Ferrazzi,** Best-Selling Author of *Never Eat Alone*

*"Gautam is a wonderful, loving human being who deeply cares about building authentic relationships first before engaging in any business. I highly recommend you break bread with him when the opportunity arises."*

**Raageshwari Loomba:** Singer, Actor, Motivational Speaker, Author @Penguin ♠

*"I have known Gautam personally for many years, and he is someone who is a role model for building meaningful relationships by a positive exchange of energy, and value*

creation many times over a meal. He is an entrepreneur. I highly recommend you connect with him as he loves to collaborate for a win-win."

**Surendran J:** Founder and CEO Success Gyan

"Most people talk about business networking . . . Through this book, Gautam takes networking to a whole new level as he teaches people the art of connecting . . . Networking sounds exhausting and effortful . . . Gautam makes connecting enjoyable and effortless . . . A must-read for anyone who believes in building meaningful relationships."

**Rajiv Talreja:** Best-Selling Author, Entrepreneur, and Business Coach

"Gautam is an entrepreneur who highly values building personal business relationships for long-term success. I have had the pleasure of breaking bread with him both in the Gulf and India."

**Shiv Khera:** Global Thought Leader and Author

"There is something powerful about the simplicity of combining food with relationships. For me, it's always been cooking for and with friends and contacts. It brings us back to a fundamentally human connection in a world of noise and distraction. My experiences with Gautam have *often been over food, and maybe that's why our relationship remains so strong over the years.*

*Enjoy the read, it's simply powerful."*

**Phil Bedford:** "The Rebel Networker"

# MY TOP 10 BOOKS THAT HAVE INSPIRED ME TO BREAK BREAD

| Book Title | Author |
| --- | --- |
| 1. Never Eat Alone | Keith Ferrazzi |
| 2. Success Principles | Jack Canfield |
| 3. UP Your Service | Ron Kaufman |
| 4. YES Attitude | Jeffrey Gitomer |
| 5. What Got You Here, Won't Get You There | Marshall Goldsmith |
| 6. Fish Philosophy | Stephen C. Lundin / Harry Paul |
| 7. Whale Done | Ken Blanchard |
| 8. Lead or Bleed | Rajiv Talreja |
| 9 Good to Great | Jim Collins |
| 10. Eat that Frog | Brian Tracy |

Lightning Source UK Ltd.
Milton Keynes UK
UKHW021015210820
368606UK00012B/1057